ASPERGER HUH?

A child's perspective

BY ROSINA G. SCHNURR, PH.D.

ILLUSTRATED BY
JOHN STRACHAN

©Anisor Publishing 1999
ISBN 0-9684473-0-9

First edition 1999

Canadian Cataloguing in Publication Data

Schnurr, Rosina G.
Asperger's, huh? : a child's perspective

ISBN 0-9684473-0-9
1. Asperger's disorder. 2. Asperger's disorder--
Juvenile literature. I. Title.

RJ506.A9S34 1998   618.92'8982 C98-901261-1

Illustrated by John Strachan

Layout & Design by Intrepid Communications

Printed & Bound in Canada by DocuLink International

Rosina G. Schnurr, Ph.D., F.A.Cl.P. is a clinical psychologist who has worked with children for over twenty years. Her experience as well as her positive and sensitive style reflect her caring concern for these special children.

John Strachan is a cartoonist and illustrator who has published works in a variety of media. He lives and works in Ottawa with his wife and two children.

This book is dedicated to
all my special young friends
who have Asperger's Disorder.

Asperger's Huh?

The Mystery

Something was wrong. Again.

My mom was crying. Again.

My dad was talking about seeing another doctor. Again.

I knew they were talking about me. Again.

I just don't get it . . . again.

We had just come home from a restaurant. It was supposed to be a celebration. My dad got this new job. My dad is an important person. I don't really know what he does but sometimes I see him on television. Anyway, a whole lot of people were there; mostly friends of my mom and dad and some of the people that my dad works with. I was the only kid. I do have a younger brother but my parents made him stay with a sitter. I'm almost 11 so I got to go.

The meal was okay. It took forever. Then my mom whispered to me that there were going to be "toasts". I thought we were going to have breakfast. I told her that I wasn't hungry. It turns out that a "toast" is when someone gets up with their wine glass and says something about my dad and then everyone touches glasses with each other and then drinks. Some "toast". Well, this went on for awhile and I was getting really bored. Then it hit me! I could make a toast too!

I stood up and talked about how my dad doesn't spend enough time with me. Then I started talking about the weather. My mom made me sit down. My dad made a joke about the weather that I didn't understand but some people laughed. We went home pretty soon after that.

But it didn't end there. When we got home, my brother saw my mom crying. He asked me if I'd done something stupid again. I hit him. He hit me back. Our dad grabbed both of us and marched us up to our rooms. They think that I can't hear them talking, but I can because I opened my door.

Another Doctor

Well, here I am in ANOTHER doctor's office. I don't know how many different doctors I've seen. I didn't want to come. I even tried to throw a tantrum but my dad wasn't in a mood to fool around. My mom says that the doctor isn't going to give me needles or anything. He, who turned out to be a she, was just going to talk to me. I've heard about those psycho doctors. You go to see them when you're crazy. I'm not crazy. At least I don't think so.

Anyway, this lady doctor is okay. She didn't make me stand on one foot or wiggle my fingers or do anything dumb. All she did was ask me some questions, mainly about school and friends and stuff. I lied about having friends and told her that I didn't really care about having friends. And she actually listened to me talk. I know I talk too much and people don't want to listen, but she did. Then she made another appointment with my parents. I don't have to come for the next appointment. I guess that means that I'm not crazy after all.

My parents went the next week and the week after that I had to go again. We all sat in a little room and the doctor started talking about "Asperger's Disorder". I said "Huh?" My parents looked just like they do whenever they meet one of my teachers. Their faces look worried and they nod their heads seriously. I was getting scared. What was this "Asperger's Disorder"? What was wrong with me? The doctor smiled her nice smile and said that there was nothing "wrong" with me but that I was a little "different" from other children. She also said that I wasn't crazy. That made me feel a lot better. Now I was really listening.

The doctor explained that in 1944 a German doctor, whose name was Hans Asperger, noticed that some of the children that he saw were different from other children of the same age. He studied them and tried to help them. Later other doctors also saw children like this and worked to help them too. Soon they began to call the differences that they saw in these children "Asperger's Disorder".

So what was different? I guess I still had my "huh?" expression on my face because the doctor just kept smiling and talking. Many things were different, she said, but the most important one, because it made a lot of children unhappy, was that children with Asperger's Disorder have a lot of difficulty making friends and having fun with other children. Also, they get upset easily about things that bother them. I knew that was like me but I never knew it had a name. My mom got up and hugged me. My dad had this sort of sad smile on his face. He put his hand on my shoulder and thanked the doctor a lot.

The Funny Thing About Friends

When we got home, my mom talked to me about "social" things like making friends. She said that it is because, with Asperger's, you have trouble understanding emotions and feelings. That means understanding what other children mean when they say certain things and what other children mean when they do certain things. It also means that other children do not understand what you say and do sometimes.

I know I really want to have friends but it never seems to work out. Most times I don't care because it is more fun to spend time by myself doing my "own thing", like drawing pictures of weather maps. My parents say I cannot spend all my time doing this even if I like it a lot.

Sometimes other children are not kind. They will play tricks on children who have Asperger's Disorder because they know that they can fool us. My mom knows a little girl who was riding a school bus but got off at the wrong bus stop because the other children on the bus told her it was her stop. She felt pretty awful when the bus pulled away and she saw the other children laughing. She felt especially awful because she did not know where she was and had to walk and walk until some nice adult helped her.

The main problem playing with other children is that they are not interested in playing what you like and you don't want to play anything else. Also, when I play, I like to always play in the same way every time. Other children want to play things their way. This upsets me and I usually get angry at them or just leave and play my own way.

My mom says it has to do with **"flexibility"**. That means being able to change from one thing to another without getting upset. A lot of times that is hard for me because I like to do things in a particular way—like when I take my bike to the park, I always go the same route. Also it is hard for me because I really, really am interested in only a few things and I want others to listen to me and to be interested in my things all the time.

By being flexible, my mom means that I can't do "my things" all the time; that I have to change to doing other things or doing things in a different way. I am getting better at this but I still don't feel very comfortable being "flexible". At least now I don't have tantrums about it. I only did that when I was a little kid.

Social Sillies

My mom also talks a lot about "social skills". I call them social sillies. That's about how much sense they make to me. What my mom means is that you have to behave in certain ways with other people. First, you must be polite. When you meet people, you must look them in the eye and smile and say "hello" or "how do you do" or shake their hand or something like that. It's called a "greeting". It was hard for me to look at people but my parents made me do it over and over and over. Now it is not so bad. I've discovered that people really like it when you smile. I don't know why but they do.

And, of course, you can't be "aggressive". No hitting, pushing, shoving and all that bad stuff. When I was in grade one, I used to like to swing at school during recess. If there was someone else on the swing, I would just push them off so that I could swing. My teacher said I was "aggressive". My parents told me I had to "share" the swing. But I couldn't. Then my dad put up a swing in our back yard and that was the only place that I was allowed to swing. I don't care so much about swinging anymore.

Along with being polite, you have to have good "hygiene". That means, you have to remember to brush your teeth, comb your hair and wash a lot. You also can't wear the same clothes every day. My mom helps me with this. She picks my clothes and makes me follow a list in the bathroom so that I don't forget to do all the necessary things. When I was little, she used to have a picture of a toilet on the list. Now she doesn't have to remind me of those stupid things.

In order to be sociable, you can't stay in your room all day. My parents try to get me to call a friend to play but I make up excuses. Sometimes, they telephone friends for me. Then I have to play with them.

If you have any little habits like blinking your eyes or rubbing your nose, try not to do them in public. I have to stop myself from making little noises in my throat whenever I'm around people. My mom calls it grunting but it is just a habit that feels good and is hard to stop. She says that I can grunt all I want in my room. Sometimes I do.

You also have to watch what you say. Of course you can't say bad words, at least not out loud. My parents don't say anything if I mumble to myself or say some in my head.

There are lots of things about talking that you have to remember. First, don't talk too much, especially if it is all about one thing. My mom says that I can only say four things about the weather and I can't ask any questions. I may make a statement about the weather being hot, cold, rainy, or windy. I can't talk about cold fronts or temperatures or anything like that.

Asking questions can get you into lots of trouble, especially asking "personal" questions, and especially asking STRANGERS "personal" questions. When I was little and I was at a shopping mall with my mom, I saw a man without hair on top of his head. I had never seen that before. So I asked the man to take off his head so that I could look at it. I couldn't see it way up there. My mom and the man laughed but later my mom told me that the man couldn't take his head off. I didn't understand that because the head of my teddy bear comes off. When I discovered that I couldn't take off my head or mom's head, I understood why they were laughing. Anyway, most of the time it is a lot safer to just make simple statements and not ask questions.

Another big "no no" are jokes. Don't even try to tell them. Other kids will just laugh at you. Somehow, I never get it right. I can't seem to get my voice to go up and down at the right times. And then I always mess up the punch line. Sometimes I can't stop myself from laughing before I get to the punch line and then all the kids end up laughing at me. When I do get to the end of the joke, nobody thinks it's funny.

Well, there they are — the social sillies. A real pain at times, but necessary.

The Weather Weebie

I want to tell you about one of my interests. I like it so much that I have a hard time when I try to stop thinking about it and talking about it. It is the weather. I know that everyone talks about the weather but not like me. I am really, really, REALLY interested in the weather.

My dad got me some information from the weather office and it was neat. There were maps and all sorts of numbers. The first thing I do in the morning when I wake up is turn on my radio and listen to the forecast. I have to set my alarm for five minutes after seven because the weather is announced at about ten minutes after seven. Once I missed it and once it did not come on until twenty-two minutes after seven. When it is not on time, it upsets me but I am learning to be patient and wait. My mom says that if I miss it, I can always ask her or my dad.

I don't want to get out of bed until I have heard the forecast and sometimes that makes me a bit late for breakfast. My mom doesn't like that because it causes a rush for everyone else. Once I'm up, I dress really quickly so that I can go downstairs and see the weather maps on TV. I also check the thermometer outside the kitchen window and the barometer that my dad and I installed on the wall just beside the kitchen window. Sometimes I even call up the "weather line" on the telephone. Just for fun, I like to listen to it three or four times.

My parents say that it's okay to be interested in the weather but all of this is "too much". So I must learn not to check the weather so often. Now I only listen to the weather line once and only if I have time.

I also must learn not to talk about the weather all the time. In other words, I have to be "flexible". Then maybe the other kids won't call me the "Weather Weebie". At first I though it was a good name. But then they started making jokes about the weather that I didn't understand. That didn't feel very good. Once, at school, they told me it was raining when it was supposed to be sunny so I rushed to the window to look and then the whole class laughed. I also hide my umbrella now so that the bigger boys can't take it and play catch with it over my head. My mom got me an umbrella that folds up really small. It's easy to hide.

Sports and Klutzes

There are other things about Asperger's Disorder that are important to know—like about sports. Sometimes children with Asperger's are not very good at sports. Other children call you "klutzy". That means that you don't run very well or very fast and sometimes you fall or drop things.

My parents say that they don't expect me to be like my brother who is good at sports. They say that being good at sports for him is like my being good at reading weather maps. My brother can't tell a cold front from a warm front and besides, he isn't even interested. Sometimes he goes out of the house without wearing his jacket or hat even though I've told him it's going to be cold. My parents make him wear proper clothes. He doesn't like that.

The other problem with sports is "teams". When you have Asperger's, you can get lost on a team. There are so many rules and things change so quickly that it's hard to know what to do and when to do it. Then your teammates get annoyed with you because you weren't in the right place at the right time or you did something that you weren't supposed to do.

I once played on a softball team. I wasn't very good at catching the ball or running, so the coach put me out in the field. He told me that if any balls came my way, I was to throw them to the pitcher. But when I did that, the team got upset because I was really supposed to throw the ball to first base to get the other team's player out. The coach explained that if it was easy to throw the ball to first base and a runner was coming to first base, then I should throw it there rather than to the pitcher.

So the next time I picked up the ball, which fell just behind second base, I threw it to first base. The team got upset again because apparently, I was supposed to throw it to second base to get out the other team's player there before throwing it to first base or to the pitcher. Besides, I didn't throw it very well and the other team ended up scoring a run.

I was getting really confused and feeling terrible. I didn't understand why the other kids were so upset. The coach seemed mad too. I was glad when my parents said that I didn't have to play a team sport anymore. Now I go swimming and I even have my very own instructor. At first I didn't like getting into the water but now it's okay. Soon I hope to learn how to swim.

Am I Smart or What?

I have to go to school like any other kid. I like school but I wish all the other children weren't there. They bother me. My teacher is nice though. I like her. My parents explained "Asperger's" to her. She knows how much I like the weather. She also knows that I talk a lot. It's okay because we have a deal. Whenever I am talking too much, she lets me know by pulling on her ear if she is at the front of the room or tapping on my shoulder if she is close to me.

My teacher even tells me that I am smart. Some kids call me "dumb" and "stupid" and "weird". I heard her talking to another teacher once who thought that I was "odd". She explained that I was not odd but just a little "different" from other children. That was when I knew that she was my friend.

The thing about school is that some parts are really easy and other parts are hard. I remember when I was in kindergarten and I could read. Everyone told me how intelligent I was. But I felt really dumb when I had to tie my shoe laces. I still can't tie them. It frustrates me so much that my mom and dad had to get me shoes that close with Velcro.

That's okay because my mom says that there is always a way around things. What she means is that when I have trouble with something, it is always possible to do the same thing another way so that I won't get so upset. She calls it being **"adaptable"**. It really means that if I CANNOT change, then the things around me CAN change. But I have to try really hard to change first.

Recess isn't too much fun. Nobody wants to play with me. I sort of hang around the other kids and pretend to be having fun. When I was a little kid and I really really liked bugs, I used to play "bug" at recess. I would get down on the ground and crawl around. No one wanted to play with me. My teacher told me that it was not **"appropriate"** to pretend to be a bug. She gave me some paper and said that it was "appropriate" for me to draw pictures of bugs crawling around. The other kids thought my pictures of bugs were pretty neat and the science teacher told me that I was very clever about bugs.

The tricky part is knowing what is appropriate and what is not appropriate. My teacher is really good about that. She never gets mad at me but she will tell me if she sees me doing something "inappropriate". Anyway, the best thing about recess is when the bell rings to go back into the school.

I have a good memory. All the teachers think it's "amazing". That makes me feel good. I can remember things like big words and long sentences. It's strange that I can read more and faster than anyone in my class but when the teacher asks me questions about what I have read, I don't get the answers right. I can repeat the words but she wants me to explain them and that's hard to do. That's why I go to see a special resource teacher on Mondays and Thursdays of every week. She is a nice lady and I try to work hard for her.

Anxiety Busters

Whew! What a day. I'm beginning to feel better now that I'm doing my "anxiety busters". They help me get rid of things like bad days. Today was awful. I missed the weather report because some dummy was going on and on about the stock market, whatever that is. Then I was late for breakfast and couldn't watch the TV weather. When I went to go out the door, I couldn't find my umbrella and I would not get on the school bus without it. My dad was upset but he drove me to school.

Even with a ride, I was still late and had to go to the principal's office by myself because my dad wasn't able to stay with me. I was scared and confused. My anxiety was getting worse and worse. I was feeling really tense. Then I got sent back to my class and the other kids had already started so I didn't know what to do and I just couldn't handle that. I started to cry. The other kids looked at me like I was a silly baby. The teacher talked to me though and that made me feel better.

Then it was recess time and a new student teacher thought we should all play "cooperative games". I got it all wrong and she said I wasn't cooperating. That's not true. I really was trying hard to do what she said. My mom had to come and get me at lunch time.

Now I'm at home and doing my "anxiety busters". They are exercises that you do to get rid of things like bad days. I have a book with pictures showing exactly how to do each one. What you do are "starts and stops" (that's what I call them). You "start" by squeezing up some part of your body really hard and then you count to five and then you "stop". The part of your body that was squeezed up then relaxes and you feel better. You do it all over your body. I follow the pictures in the book and count exactly to five each time.

The next thing I'm going to do is look for my umbrella. My Grannie is here with me and she is good at finding things. I am going to put my umbrella in my bed so it will be there for tomorrow morning. Grannie even said she would make me chocolate chip cookies and I could eat them while I watch the weather channel. I really like my Grannie.

Little Things, Big Things

Another thing to know about Asperger's Disorder is that sometimes little things bother you a lot. Like when you put something in one place, where it should be, and then someone moves it. I used to play with leggo blocks a lot when I was a little kid. I always arranged them in the same pattern and then my little brother would come along and mess them up. I would get so upset that I would whack him and then I would really get into trouble. My parents took away my leggo blocks. Mom said that if I could not change, then the environment needed to change. I didn't understand that for a long time but I do now. My mom was making me be 'adaptable'.

Sometimes big things bother you, like noises. I still do not like the sound of the vacuum cleaner. When I was little, I used to scream until mom turned it off. The sound was just too much. My mom solved the problem though. She bought me earphones and now I listen to music while she vacuums.

Speaking of noises, I can make the sound of the microwave beeps. Sometimes I try to fool my mom. Usually she just laughs. She only gets annoyed when I keep doing it over and over. It feels good to make noises and sometimes it is hard to stop making them.

Another 'little' thing that can turn into a 'big' thing happens when you try to fix something to make it right. My dad and I went to the hardware store to get a light bulb and when we passed the nails, they were all messed up. They should have been in their right boxes. My dad said "don't worry about it" and "forget it". But I knew the nails should be in their right boxes so I found the store manager and told him to fix it.

That's how a little thing like a nail can turn into a big thing like my dad getting upset and the store manager getting upset and then we didn't even get the light bulb and that made my mom upset. I still don't understand why it was such a big deal. Anyway, my dad calls me the "Great Correcter" and sometimes the "Police Patrol". What I do know is that when my dad says to "forget" something, I try to hurry past or not to look so that it won't bother me and then I won't get into trouble.

You and Who Else?

If you have Asperger's Disorder, you are not the only person in the world. Other children may have Asperger's too. You won't know it when you meet them because it does not show like a cast on a broken arm. Also, boys are more likely than girls to have it. I don't know if that makes us more special or not.

I know another boy who comes to play with me while our moms talk. They met at a "support group". That's a bunch of people who talk to each other and try to help each other. My mom hasn't been crying so much since she started going there. Anyway, Michael is a chess freak. He even plays chess with himself. He doesn't talk as much as me. It is like he is thinking all the time. I draw maps while he plays chess. Our moms say this isn't really playing together but at least we don't fight.

Another reason that you are not alone is that you might have a relative who has Asperger's too. I remember that the doctor said that sometimes you can find male relatives in your family who are like you. In my family, my Uncle Lewis, who is my dad's brother, is a lot like me. He talks a lot, mainly about his work. He became an engineer because he always liked wires and things. You should see his collection of wires. Now, THAT'S weird.

So What's Important?

The most important thing to remember when you have Asperger's Disorder is that you are a good and okay person. You just see the world a little differently. Sometimes you don't understand things and sometimes you misunderstand things. Also, you likely have some habits that bug other people.

But none of this is your fault and it is not a reason for others to laugh at you or dislike you. Unless, of course, you are nasty to them. What you have to remember is that they probably don't even know about Asperger's. My advice is don't try to explain it to them. You'll probably get it all mixed up and then they still won't understand but they'll think that you're really weird. If you really want someone to know about Asperger's, ask one of your parents or a teacher to help explain it.

Another thing that is really important is that you have some people that you can **trust** to explain things to you. '**Trust**' means that they will always tell you the truth and help you. When you feel upset and you don't know why, talk to your mom or dad or a teacher. They can help you to understand better about "feelings" and can help you find ways to make a situation much better.

And, remember to be **FAAT**! Or at least try to be.

Flexible – Try to change

Adaptable – If you can't change, try to change what is around you

Appropriate – The right thing at the right time

Trust someone – Mom, Dad, Teacher

Asperger's Huh?

Yes, I think I have Asperger's figured out. Now I don't go "huh?" so much. It's really very simple. Asperger's is just like having only a FEW pieces of a puzzle and trying to put it together right. You need to have ALL the pieces and sometimes you need help to put them together right.

For each copy of Asperger's Huh?, send $20.00* to:
(Canada and United States only)

Anisor Publishing
P.O. Box 46130, 2339 Ogilvie Road
Gloucester, Ontario,
Canada, K1J 9M7

You may photocopy this page.   **(shipping and handling included in Canada and U.S.A.)*
Tel.: 613-741-1115   Fax: 613-745-2875

-- -- -- ✂ --

Anisor Publishing, P.O. Box 46130, 2339 Ogilvie Road., Gloucester, Ontario, Canada, K1J 9M7

Please send _____ copies of **Asperger's, Huh?** to:

Name: _____

Address: _____ *Apt:* _____

City: _____ *Prov/State:* _____ *PC/ZIP:* _____

Country: _____ *Tel:* (_____) _____

I have enclosed $20.00 per copy. *(Cheque or Money Order, svp)* ☐

-- -- -- ✂ --

Anisor Publishing, P.O. Box 46130, 2339 Ogilvie Road., Gloucester, Ontario, Canada, K1J 9M7

Please send _____ copies of **Asperger's, Huh?** to:

Name: _____

Address: _____ *Apt:* _____

City: _____ *Prov/State:* _____ *PC/ZIP:* _____

Country: _____ *Tel:* (_____) _____

I have enclosed $20.00 per copy. *(Cheque or Money Order, svp)* ☐